Old Snow, White Sun

Praise for *Old Snow, White Sun*

Caroline Goodwin's latest work invited me in to hear of intimate things, of how she's met with others, of lives and deaths, and being around with humans, plants and creatures in this world. It gave me glimpses of her experience: journeys, visions, moments of everyday life with friends, companions, grandmother, mother, loss, and all that difficult stuff, with Love at the heart of it, all the while incantating things and powers (thoughts are things) in a way she has made her own.

These energies are born of an urgent, implicit questioning—not just about where we are these days with the great non-human planet, but given that dislocation, and an overwhelming yearning for the old connection—how do we get on with it? Get on with one another? Nowadays a Heron is at once a beautiful bird, an addictive drug and a high-tech warplane: these poems say: okay then, if you really want to listen, this is how that feels.

—Graham Hartill, author of *Rhapsodies* and *Cennau's Bell*

Acknowledgements

"Telluride," *sugared water 008,* forthcoming.

"Not, I'll Not" sequence, *The Dewdrop,* March 2020 and *Without a Doubt: Poems Illustrating Faith,* New York Quarterly Anthology, forthcoming.

"Antiphony," *South Dakota Review,* volume 55 no. 4, 2021.

"I'm Happy to Drive You All the Way Home," *Atlanta Review,* Vol. XXVI, No. 1, Fall/Winter 2019.

"In a Time of Mourning," *Panhandler Magazine,* February 2019.

The following poems were published in the 2015 chapbook, *Peregrine,* by Finishing Line Press, Georgetown, KY, 2015: "The Visitor", "The Mechanics", "Star Set," "The Lacnunga," "Coleoptera," and "Nine Herbs Charm".

"Nine Herbs Charm" first appeared online in *Monday Night Lit,* September 2014.

Old Snow, White Sun

Poems

Caroline Goodwin

JACKLEG PRESS

JackLeg Press
www.jacklegpress.org

Copyright © Caroline Goodwin 2021.
Published by JackLeg Press.
All rights reserved.
Printed in the United States of America.

ISBN- 978-1-7373307-8-3

No part of this work may be reproduced or utilized in any form or by any means, electronic or mechanical, including photocopying, microfilm, and recording, or by any information storage and retrieval system, without permission in writing from the publisher.

Library of Congress Cataloging-in-Publication Data

Cover design by Richard Every.
Cover image *The Power of Prayer* by Sarah Finney.

Dedications

For Naomi Louise and Isabel Neva, my lights and loves, my worlds.

In memory of Josephine Neville Goodwin.

Many thanks to Jen Harris and JackLeg Press, for believing in this book, and to Finishing Line Press for publishing *Peregrine*.

For longstanding poetry friendship and support, my gratitude to Hugh Behm-Steinberg, Rebekah Bloyd, Nan Cohen, Donna de la Perrière, Melissa Eleftherion, Linda Janacek, Sarah Kobrinsky, Joseph Lease, Christina Lloyd, Denise Newman, Lisa Rosenberg, and Tanu Wakefield.

And, as always, with all my heart, for Nick.

—We are each a lens;

Some nights the world is made of gazes
peering through me as I sit here

under her. I pretend she
understands, but she and many

of these stars are dead. Their light
is not for me and is not her.

—Stephanie Bolster, "Portrait of Alice as the Poet's
Universe" from *White Stone: The Alice Poems*

When logic and proportion
Have fallen sloppy dead—

And the White Knight is talking backwards
And the Red Queen is "off with her head!"

Remember what the dormouse said:
"Feed your head. Feed your head."

—Jefferson Airplane, "White Rabbit"

Contents

Oriar
  In A Time of Mourning   1
  Not, I'll Not   7
  Not, I'll Not (2)   8
  Not, I'll Not (3)   9
  Antiphony   10

Mothlight
  Ring-Billed Gull   19
  The Mechanics   20
  Star Set   22
  The Lacnunga   26
  Coleoptera   34
  Nine Herbs Charm   35
  Secondhand News   44
  Unreadable Book That Will Not Close   45

Epiphytic
  Telluride   53
  Loves Me Not   54
  I'm Happy to Drive You All the Way Home   55
  Perennial   56
  I'm Happy to Listen to Your Version of Things   57
  Quill   59
  I'm Happy to Collaborate with The Artist(s)   60
  Epiphytic   62

Notes   71
Bio   73

Oriar

In A Time of Mourning

for Bruce Carl Edenso (May 9, 1956 – June 22, 2017)

i.

Once, in a time of mourning, I was awake all night.
It was an equinox. It was how the common loon made
a thumbprint on the lake. The porcupine a companion.
After drinking, I crawled underneath the covers
    and got warm.
Your voice the color of crow feathers. Your voice
    a tough stem.
When the traveler came with a basket, it was green
    and sawtoothed.
It was filled with petals and quills. And although I floated
for a while untethered, the wind was swift-footed.
It was the one force that held me to the lake. When
the time came, I was still awake. I was awake for you.
And the light grew stronger, a pair of swans. I was awake
for you, for a very thin covering of snow. I was awake
    and we walked.

ii.

Take it up with God, who of course is a mere bell
    tinkling in the alleyway. In a pile of skins.

  Streetlamp and bluefin, where the traveler opens
    his coat. Not bury myself up to the neck.

Not question the trajectory, make an assumption
    (when you reach for my shoes

before dawn, I will not resist). An old star is blowing itself
    out. Can you hear it? Buzzing through the grate.

I'll not crush the kernel underfoot, not ask for the reasons
    or even your most valuable shirt. I'll drive.

Fuck sake! Iron, matchstick, creosote, rip-rap, nemesia,
    blood feather, birch bark, aggregate fruit.

iii.

Crawls up out of the cave in increments.
That which all afternoon formed a pale borealis.
I held out one hand, one sleeve. Take
that. Cat on my lap. Light in the cypress.
Glacier blue, the night in ceramics.
What comfort, your fur and linen,
blown glass. Shards of the tinted eye, bits
of the hand rising. The hand like an aster.
The hand and the hand and the hand
a cut branch. Your cosmos, your embrace
a brushstroke of stars, a kaleidoscope
I could never have imagined.

iv.

Wear that cloak of scars. Lay out the incense,
    the sage wand, the final horn. After a time,

a catkin makes its way through the cracks.
    In the street: a child, a snowdrift extending

itself. A coolness over the throat.
    A cool arm. When my breath rises

in white blossoms, the Matanuska River
    is the turning glacier, blue and grinding,

is a chamber of silt. Just dip in a finger. That
    which splits and binds, that which is woolly,

that which reveals its tusk. Don't say I didn't warn you.
    That which the vision lays at the foot.

I cup my father in my palms. His leather
soles, his skinny arms. And my mother,
whose lungs I plucked from the old willow,
whose forgiveness I long for but will never obtain.
Whose heartbreak is a wintergreen or candystick.
Thereafter, my brothers in their finery
cured and crusted with salt. And the dog
with her gleaming pelt. What a funny little
tribe, don't you think? When we walk together
now of course there is paintbrush, twayblade,
primrose, heather, vetch. Look closely, my love,
at the map on my forehead, on my neck.

vi.

Now done, now dark, now the facts
    about flames. In the Napa Valley: Stag's

Leap Winery, White Rock, Vinroc, Paradise Ridge.
    If I'd believed this could happen, I would have

found a way. And, waking early, would have warned you:
    star lily, knotweed, standing on the corner, the night

you offered me your heart. Out came the first
    emergency vehicles, flashing lights. What

if I said *I love you?* Water takes the shape of its container.
    Affection takes the shape of its water. The fires

have claimed their 43rd victim. And what did I see?
    A cake of soap, a half-sour pickle. The side
of your face.

Not, I'll Not

Lay a lion limb. Tie up the branch, ask
    too soon for the ring or even

for the word. In the rushes, explosions. When
    we rediscover one another,

the hill takes on unseemly proportions.
    Grows by spreading. By a frond, by

a tower of jewels. At some point, the lobed
    or divided leaves of the violet. The loved.

The swarm of blue bottles and even
    a cluster of tiny antennae. In the swaying

grasses, I heard all the voices: *too late, too late,*
    too late, the tilting room, the silver anklet.

Not, I'll Not (2)

Feast on thee. All the way to Yellowknife,
    all the way to the lake. The word

was *awen,* the word was *fish.* I pronounced the word
    to you in the musk ox room at eventide,

under the quilt. At YouTube headquarters,
    the shooter came out on her knees.

On her curlew, muskrat, bittern, anemone
    bulb and fin. When I carry the wooden

bowl, it's your hand. When I fall, when I
    burn out to the rising sun, O Lord,

O flannel shirt, O salmon leather, fireside chat. I'll be
    the one on the sidewalk rolling up the fragrant leaves.

Not, I'll Not (3)

Be heron, be oblivion. Where you at? If I push
   the wheel: suffering. If I speak the dreams

of others (others) if I hold you tight and light
   up the rose fountain, break the sky?

Will you come to me then, blue skull, be me,
   be mine? Indeed, there will be time after dark

for the silver owl, the seawall, green paint. My breath
   along the waterway, how it finds you, opens

the pistil and ovary, the ornamental rush. I
   am the one you've been waiting for.

All this time. I am the pasture and sedge, turning
   and turning under the fences, light.

Antiphony

i.

The deeper the knowledge, the greater the mystery.
After a long afternoon, you lean in close and speak:
blue, blue as it ever will be. In the alleyway, snails.
In the raised garden, tiny flags. When a hundred
gold frogs make themselves known and another
child taps at the glass, you take me underground
and place the lyric in my hands. *Paperwhite. Narcissus.*
Turn me to wire, wrap me up in rags. You understand
that wayfaring sleeper in the doorway. The manner in which
a helping hand arrives (four-legged or winged)
and the light calls out from every direction. As well
belonging to me, cool water coming down.

ii.

Here in shadow the crustacean,
with its one crushing claw,
beckons and travels
under and under – (where the news)
and fills me with night––-
me the girl bent at the waist the girl
reclining in a bed of skins (or trash)
and you don't see me or even register
my voice which I admit is like a pin
or a slim appendage or a stamen curling
around some other entity: *here*
the grass basket the string of seeds---

iii.

Dawn rises up again, perplexed. A man
who knows where the carnivals are. Once
upon a time: North Beach, Steel Pulse,
jacaranda, white-crowned sparrow. I stand
on the corner for a long time, fingering
the turquoise ring. When I see your face,
I set foot in the street. *The power of love.*
The power of love. At the underground shop,
a woman becomes visible, along with a hundred
other names I want to speak, or simply to remember.
But ah, but oh what bright lichen takes root
on my tongue. What sunbeams of muscle.

iv.

Not the man with his head back,
ecstatic with the nearness of Creation. Not
your eye turned gold with sunrise. Not entering
the museum to find our fathers scraping
colors from the mountainside, repeating
these words: *banner, flag*. None of this
did I offer you at the time of my crossing, none
of it. The myrtle has glossy aromatic foliage.
The homeland is an unbroken plain.
It is cut by several major rivers. When I stick
my small needle into the eardrum, I expect
a good drop of your blood. Evidence of pain.

v.

The ebbtide, hemlock, horsetail,
sacred mollusk, crusty seashell, halfway
house and railroad and chunks of seafoam
and one or another glass bead. What I believe
love can erase, or replace: I line it all up
on the sill. Come along now, old friend.
We're almost there. What sparkles green
finds its way into the vessels, into the jars
of preserves on the grandparents' shelves.
When a man grows tired he hangs up his hat.
When he steals my name, I slumber.
Too soon, too late. Every brittle star in the sea.

vi.

Be the nocturne played haltingly.
Lie in wait where I'm nothing but breath.
Settle in the aftermath, a coat of dust.
Send out my roots, small thoughts or tumbleweed.
Abandon my belief, the ticking heart.
Follow the northern flicker, its rattling pretense.
The sinewy hand. The mask of the somnambulist,
shining blue glaze, daisy chain. Tonight
the sky's a glowing silver and my dread
a certain possession. O I will leave this
beautiful place. I will depart with the shark
and the seal. I will forget.

Mothlight

Ring-Billed Gull

The grass is visible again. And the stones. When morning
    arrives at the mountaintop, there is the glacier, there are
        my eyelids.

Carrion bird, clacking beak. Deer leg, vertebrae. My love,
    I do not begrudge you that simplicity. Do not avoid the
        reflection

of the egret in the lake or the sandhill crane. I promise
    I can gather it up now, one method by which the past is
        filigree. Is the ring-billed

gull, is blue smoke pooling in the cave.

The Mechanics

for Tony and Dustin

in the bottom of the bag   in
    the glass in the bottle

in the starlight and the smallest
    constellation   in the soft gills

in the underside of the frond
    in the hank of black beads

in the melody rising from the meadow
    folded and coming up again

amphibious pearly throat
    in the screw gun and the wrench

in the satellite over the beach
    spokes of the wheel and flat screen

in the sand sliding under us   in the
    sand falling over us   fine as flour

in the paw print and arrowhead
    at the end of the lane   in the foxglove

in the circle of dust   in the object
     at rest   in the shade in the surf

in the vector traveling north   a kitchen
     table   a blue cloth and cypress

green as jade   in the pivot and the radius
     in the smoke rolling down

in the centipede   the iridescent
     sensation of all its legs

in the tent pitched in a bright meadow
     in the breeze   in the firelight

that warmed us   orange and red   in
     momentum   in the moth head

in the death head   in the talons of the owl
     in the folds of cloth   where we found it

where we left it   lying in its finery
in its wrecked wings

Star Set

for Anne

folded my regrets
paper fortunes
placed them in my pocket
with the beach glass
with the jade

with the words and how
much longer

how much redder the sun
your shining hair your
long-stemmed wine glass
upside-down on the tray

when the news
there was too
much between us

the skyscraper
the wires and mirrors
how to kick it all aside

kick the sky filling
with torn clouds
the dry grain
and the cells

kick the net of electricity
the quarry and live oak
the leaf and burl

and the tenets of the covenant
and those who so quickly
abandoned
the shore

this precision this
origami swan

a memory in each
of my fingertips
an elegant silver fork
on a plate   a pair of shoes

in the room

delicate skin of the upper arm
gold rim on the edge of the page
who came knocking
who broke down the door

sit back in the weeds
full of my body
full of the night sky

faraway
beach lighting
my ribcage

dust at my feet
one green stone and

the branches
of the stars

The Lacnunga

for Todd

i.

straw god, painted skull, high window

the key belief of the spiritualists was that
"thoughts are things"

are the charms and the bones
are the beads and the leaves
are the lines and the patio

garden-like, full of plants

ii.

when the ocean rose over the aleutians
you were making your lunch and i
was making my lunch

cancer patients are asked to calm their minds
and to vividly picture their cancers

we could hear the water
but it wasn't so loud
it wasn't so cold   there
was nothing to be afraid of and

we spoke over the point of land

iii.

silverberry, couchgrass, put up your feet

we won't fully understand what happened here
until time has had a chance to filter that out for us

until the charm, until the garlic, leek and English daisy

light coming up off the ocean

until the law until the reflection the barbed wire
until the itinerant medium the staple the poison
the newborn baby in your arms   until the limelight

have you ever
been up
to the fence?

iv.

when i was a girl in alaska we walked to the ravine behind
the quik stop and hurled glass bottles against the rock wall
and laughed out loud for a long time when they shattered

v.

as we picture you   as we reminisce   as the painted skull   as
you are standing on the stage   your performance   some
trick of our fractured memory   the bales of straw the light
in your face   in the ferris wheel and the empty beach   (in
your face)   you are alone at the Laramie Circle K   you are
holding the gas nozzle the sky is wide you are afraid   what
happened here, the culture that caused this   each
compartment   each knot of wire   each light a coiled spring
the waves and your heart and along the stretch of beach the
wheel turning forward (turn back now) and away

vi.

in the same vein the patients are to imagine
the natural healing forces of their body
like heroic knights defeating the dragon of cancer
to picture themselves fully well and happy

vii.

in the same vein as the fox
in the field   in the same
bright grasses   closing over
our eyes

viii.

to speak of the sick child   the ferris wheel
lit up at night   your feet in the water
in the sound of small waves   weak waves
little potted flower i brought to your door i think
it was a violet   your friends around you
nobody expected   it was a raucous party   it was
an enormous moon between the buildings   embarcadero
wild green parrot   telegraph   ferry building   ferries
their engines purring
they were moving
they were filled with passengers
or were they plants
we couldn't tell   they looked
so strong so stately
it could have been anything
arriving and departing   they glinted
you said   they
illuminated every face

Coleoptera

black twig   bright branch   how the berries
     accumulate   blue dish   and a moth
folded into the books   mother where
     are you hiding?   slip a needle
into the cloth   and listen   the sound of breath
     is the sound of claws on stone
and so i came into the world looking
     for a cloak   for the smell of fur
for the water on ferns   the blank sky
     one branch held out in the path
black twig   black eye   and when
     you find me?   bind the silver
bracelet carved by god and look look
     out for me in the furthest poplar
hanging my clothes up to dry

Nine Herbs Charm

i.

the wrinkled glass

    (you swept it empty)

cleaned it out

    cleaned my heart

out and far away the flight

    of the bare-throated tiger-heron

neck bent back

ii.

fury, song, heavy storm
floods communities
in western alaska--
through the green
fuse, down the yukon—
sing the charm three times
over the mouth, over
both ears

iii.

Heron 1 is an MALE (medium altitude long endurance) UAV (unmanned aerial vehicle) built for the respective theatre of operation. 2013: German Herons log 15,000 Combat Operation Hours in Afghanistan.

iv.

heron: code for heroin

v.

river, the white stones
charm, the stone bowl
blood, my black heart
bridge, your mint sprig
leaf, the crushed dust

vi.

hybrid children
watch the
sea

vii.

against a sudden/violent

      stabbing pain... shot

by witches, elves and other

      spirits that fly through the air...

acquire the feverfew, red

      nettle and plantain... boil

in butter... block the ears (loud,

      oh! were they loud/when

they rode over the hill...

viii.

Heron 1 can carry an array of sensors, including infra-red and visible-light surveillance, intelligence systems (COMINT and ELINT) and various radar systems, totaling up to 250 kg (550 lb). Heron is also capable of target acquisition and artillery adjustment.

ix.

the wrinkled glass

  the ice-white waves

the thing that should

  not be, history, apart-hood

your kettle and flame,

  my ivory tusk (open the letter:

hurricane, floodgate, levee, imagine

  our feet at the hearth

 now that the war is through with me

Secondhand News

We knew about the biggest clover in the world.
We understood the green of the Northern Lights
because it was the same green that inhabited
our blood (all year).
We drove the old truck from Fairbanks to New Orleans
(along the way we did resist the urge to count
the rows of clover).
We understood that the clover would be enjoyable,
would provide its nectar.
We arrived at the tip of the seed, American meadow.
Where, of course, we found pitchforks and euphoria.
Where we could not remain.

Unreadable Book That Will Not Close

—Roo Borson, "Mothlight"

i.

If you can see the metal sky, the plate-shaped
lilypad, the woolly bear and loon, the friend
at my heart, my forehead, both my hands

moving and reliable with a stitch now looping
through the rushes, herb mercury, spurge
family with its attending lance-shaped leaves

and a long June sunset over a northern
lake and a pair of grebes cackling:
all shapes on deck – all muted colors—

call to power, fleur-de-lis, the bog spruce will hold
out hope. When I notice the painting
I cover my eyes and a few fires blaze up

to the South. If you can hear me dream, if
you can preserve the stringed instrument
with a bit of patience, it won't be the moth poem

it won't be the rose poem, or even the hibiscus
which is the source of a black dye
that was used for varying purposes in the East

or the low, trailing, evergreen bearberry
with its waxy, urn-shaped flowers
saying *here now, hold me, hold me*

again and again. No. Look now for a thin page
with very light ink, or a pelican feather
or, better yet, a creature long extinct hatching

from the mouth of the old mine. And tell me
how it goes again, that song? Woman
at the fountain, man tipping his hat, some kind

of pledge or plea? The grebes are just that
silhouette, and the sky now a violet curtain.
Here, at the muddiest end of the marsh, I fall on my knees.

ii.

Whose ghost moves over the floor? Whose
jewel colors in the cattails? Today
there is the report of snow geese
dead on the shores of Cambridge Bay. "Too many
to count," the newsman says.

Who carried in the musk ox horns and skull?
The valuable pelt? The snowshoes?
Atlantic salmon escape into the Pacific
during a terrific windstorm.

Roethke says "any old stick, pie-tin, or pencil's
material to beat out the meter of happy bones."

I say bumblebee or a malamute in winter,
the Arctic sky, the oldest rock in the world.
I say Nunavut, Yellowknife, Tuktoyaktuk,
The Gold Range or Ragged Ass Road
or Vee Lake or a birthright of snow
or my own exhausted body in the canoe.

iii.

Horsetail makes a pleasant sound in the wind.
It is the sound of mending or of a small waterfall.
It is not the sound of the playground, or of the tetherball
chain. At the back of the house, the pallets,
the rusty nails, the place where my grandmother
sat down to rest in the rain.

iv.

At first light the water stills. And a family
of ducks, simple mallards in the green,
shaking and dipping their bills methodically,
astonishes me. Every night you held me
comes back in the rain. Every embrace
and harsh word. The fact that I continue
in my body, in this web of red lace, makes it
possible. Makes it all surrender, the heart
a door, makes your voice a refrain
for the stay-at-homes. It arrives
in the wee hours, filled with myth.
The goose barnacle is a tree that bears birds
instead of fruit. The skullcap is truly a tranquilizer.
And what, when you see me perusing the edge
of the lake, my ankle adorned with the leech?
My veins all bright blue? It is only August, so what
will it take? *The softening properties of the slippery*
elm, a lubricant to ease labor. Modern herbalists
list an extract of moccasin flower root
as a sedative, especially for nervousness,
hysteria, and anxiety accompanied by insomnia.

v.

All night the sensation in my spine, between
    the shoulder blades.
A twisting, like wool in a drop spindle.

If I could even begin to report
    the actual depth of my longing—
the hunter waits in a boat on the south side

of the Porcupine, rifle on his thighs. Where
    the river is a length of gray chain.
And these bookshelves you built me –

and a line of thin smoke climbing
    and how light comes up off the lake.
If I hold the ulu at the correct angle, I can split

fibers from the hide. At dawn
    a pair of tall birds works the shore.
They are not graceful. They cackle and squawk.

They say *lichen.* They say *caribou, muskrat.*
    will-o-the-wood, whippoorwill, walk
through the valley, common loon and whistling

swan and wolf. I say go ahead and give me your hand
    again. I say come on back through these old shadows
and reticulated fronds, through the peat, through the mute
    silt, opening your stupid wings.

Epiphytic

Telluride

    Come, book of myths.
Come tailor, come seamstress,
    come theater of dust.
Come butcher and baker

(the golden-bristled
    boar)—

When I was young I believed there was a door behind the
moon. Ursus Major, pilot light. When I hustled home from
the neighbor's house, it was nearly springtime. I couldn't
have known. He had already held my aunt down on the
bed. With the weight of his person. In the corner lot a field
of wild borage. *Ne m'oubliez pas.*

Candlestick,

this grief
a particle of moon

boring into the lung
into the eye --

Loves Me Not

At first we lay down by the blowing vines.
Next to the ditch, dragonflies.
And a small hawk bisected a cloud.
And he moved, and his breath was sure.
And maybe the river flowed backwards.
Maybe far away the river flowed backwards.
Plastic tops and strings made their way out of the brush.
And a set of gills pulsed, big friend of the stones.
An infant's body in the Ganges, a white sun. Then
all at once he was walking away I could tell I could tell.
Up the green dune to the forest of lost children.
It was dawn, it was his beautiful back,
his lovely face at the mountaintop. There
were so many others and each one loved
him. What a flame occurs in the throat.
All night I toss petals into the ditch.
All night under the stars revolving.

I'm Happy to Drive You All the Way Home

Past the great palms, the trunks gnarled up and roots buckling the sidewalk. Under the clear sky. Past the skinny boy in the Megadeth tee. The surfboards the skateboards. The barrel planters of geraniums (imagine the roly-polies underneath, blue grey, also known as woodlice or potato bugs or armadillo bugs). To the back of the valley, I'm happy to drive you. Up Reina del Mar and South Reina del Mar past Ursula, Naomi, Juanita, headed east. Past the twins playing Frisbee in the middle of the block, whose older brother may or may not be home. Pink stucco, white tile. Past the corner store (Sweeney Ridge commemorates the first sighting of the San Francisco Bay by the Portola Expedition, 1769) and maybe even up to the small cave in the hillside where I first heard the spider spinning, the mayflies, (eleoniscus), the chattering squirrel, the wren. The SF 51-C missile structure vandalized: *No Smoking in Bed*. I'm happy to drive you: daffodil, palomino, old friend, Mustang, narcissus, Golden Earring, Radar Love, Corvette. Each to each. Of course, I'm happy to tell that story to you or to myself. The one where the girl is strong enough. The one where she survives.

Perennial

for Lael

In an instant, like they
    say: *blink of an eye.*
And we stand in the light green
    foliage for a while, looking.
A favorite pair of headphones, personal effects.
    The last one to see you a clerk
at the video store. An old woman peeking
    through the shades. *As the man hours*
began to number in the thousands,
    the search evolved into a Type III.
And what moves in the tidepools: thin
    fronds of kelp like hair or branches
or willows or grasses or string. A bottlefly
    against the dirty glass. When we return
to the gardening, a storm front moves
    in from the West. Familiar wind
in the hemlocks: *not a trace.*

I'm Happy to Listen to Your Version of Things

The belted kingfisher is found year-round near quiet waters. The San Francisco area is blessed with year-round open water. The belted kingfisher builds its nest near the end of a long tunnel. The San Francisco Housing Data Hub is your go-to resource for learning about policies and programs that affect housing affordability and are administered by local government agencies in San Francisco. The small, plump dunlin is perhaps the most widespread winter shorebird in the San Francisco area. The American robin's close relationship with urban areas has allowed many residents an insight into a bird's life. The San Francisco police department badge reads *Oro en Paz—Fierro en Guerra:* Gold in Peace – Iron in War. The Osprey is commonly seen over large waterbodies from April through September. As a mourning dove bursts into flight, its wings 'clap' above and below its body for the first few wingbeats. The lance-like bill of the Marbled Godwit may look plenty long enough to reach buried worms, amphipods and small clams, but the godwit doesn't seem content with its reach. The San Francisco Planning Department's award winning, innovative and user-friendly Property Information

Map provides a single access point for a variety of useful property data, zoning and permitting information. Sharp-shinned hawks terrorize the songbirds living in San Francisco's neighborhoods. The male Anna's hummingbird is the most distinctive hummingbird in the Bay Area. The belted kingfisher builds its nest near the end of a long tunnel. The belted kingfisher is found year-round near quiet waters.

Quill

She's diurnal and her eyes a dark green.
She curls the gilded paper, watches the ironwork.
She owns a simple song, the song
which is also my grandmother's song.
Her fingertips are dry and cracked.
Her hair a big flame.
She breathes into dreams.
She befriends the silver owl.
She is the button jar, the junk drawer.
Her skin glows like the heads of wheat.
She holds the slotted tool and the needle tool
(cradles them).
Long ago, she befriended my mother.
She woke at 3:00 am and lit the kindling.
She gathered a nosegay of sweetpeas
(the melody played).
If I didn't know better, I would
ask her name. I would ask her name.

I'm Happy to Collaborate with The Artist(s)

The number of American troops killed in Afghanistan and Iraq between 2001 and 2012 was 6,488. The Cliff Swallow is the most widespread swallow in San Francisco, and you can often encounter it in the hundreds. The number of American women who were murdered by current or ex male partners between 2001 and 2012 was 11,766. If you stop to inspect the undersides of a bridge, you may see hundreds of gourd-shaped nests stuck to the pillars and structural beams. The number of American troops killed in Afghanistan and Iraq between 2001 and 2012 was 6,488. The Hermit Thrush is certainly one of the most beautiful songsters to inhabit Bay Area woodlands and forest floors. The Hermit Thrush's song lifts the soul with each note, and leaves a fortunate listener breathless at its conclusion. The number of American women who were murdered by current or ex male partners between 2001 and 2012 was 11,766. The Western Scrub-Jay is a jay of open forests, especially scrub and chaparral. This is one of the few birds able to eat hairy caterpillars. The number of American troops killed in Afghanistan and Iraq between 2001 and 2012 was 6,488. The Brown Creeper may be the most inconspicuous bird in North America. With its short, vertical hops, the Brown Creeper spirals up a rugged trunk, constantly probing the tree's wrinkled skin for hidden insect treasures. The number of American women who were murdered by current or ex male partners between 2001 and 2012 was 11,766. The turkey vulture feeds entirely on carrion, which it can sometimes detect by scent

alone. The song of the Winter Wren is distinguished by its
melodious tone and by its endurance. The number of
American troops killed in Afghanistan and Iraq between
2001 and 2012 was 6,488. Western Gulls are the only gulls
to nest in the San Francisco area, and the Farallon Islands
host between 22,000 and 25,000 pairs yearly. The number
of American troops killed in Afghanistan and Iraq between
2001 and 2012 was 6,488. The number of American
women who were murdered by current or ex male partners
between 2001 and 2012 was 11,766.

Epiphytic

for Nan

> "Once a friend said to me that wild foods are boring,
> and it would be hard to argue with her if you had to
> subsist on acorns boiled in water with ash and steamed
> fern roots."
>> —Jeffrey Greene, *In Pursuit of Wild Edibles*

i.

shreds of Spanish moss
torn flags in the juniper

at night my hands open
of themselves

and the matter that made me
is the matter with me

is cabbage and onion the size
of my brain or my fist

ii.

granular pale greenish-gray thin
water surface beyond which
lay my sister   lay my sister

every eye and chloroplast
map and tile   where the carpenter
stood on deck chanting   *what if*

my heart set sail in this body
of water   what if I claimed
your hand?   then the structure

built of snow rings
cast its wings in the hedgerow
in the zone of dust

alpenglow   my sister's voice
and the Oregon junco
keeping up the song:
go now go now go

iii.

om mani padme—silverfish!

iv.

and of course there is my aunt
at the loom   the cloud of gnats

at the pane   or is it smoke
or is it the soldier she loved

her hair the warp and woof
the skin of her wrist   blue vein

can't you hear the clock
click 'round and don't

you understand her
true root scored with flak

v.

o let me hobble
away away away

vi.

tender lichen
full sun or shade
mottled leather
stickleback
coins of light
of autumn
concentric
explosions
toadskin
jellyskin
single spore
yellow map
rock disk
felthorn
smooth horn
powder horn
grey and black
and shield
and shore

we believe could hold us steady

vii.

if he would simply
be clover/love(r)
the split stem

my celestial calendar
whose opening
received the revelation(s)'

cardinal in the eastern cedar

in the thimble
filled with honey

vii.

where mist enters
the body

where the night
ticks and expands

is the little scar he left
or the little mark

(all morning i stand
at the sink

all morning the sky
takes on the color
of blood)

viii.

the taste of apricots
    the taste of cream

the shape
    of a red setter

loping over sand
    the sun and fur

the faraway trilling
    the scent of wild iris

or nasturtium or hyacinth
    or the touch of evening

chrysanthemum   varied thrush
    white-crowned sparrow

marsh hen or swift
    or the violet-green swallow

standing at the spring
    offering the taste
        in store for us

Notes

The Nine Herbs Charm is an Old English charm recorded in the 10th century, part of the Lacnunga manuscript, the oldest written Anglo-Saxon medical text. My poem "Nine Herbs Charm" incorporates a few translated verses from the actual charm, along with lyrics from the Metallica song "The Thing That Should Not Be" and information from Wikipedia about the German Heron warplanes.

"The Lacnunga" incorporates bits of text from *The Laramie Project* and also *The Herbal Lore of Wise Women and Wortcunners* by Wolf D. Storl.

The sentences about birds in "I'm Happy to Listen to Your Version of Things" and "I'm Happy to Collaborate with the Artist(s)" are taken from the textbook *Birds of San Francisco and the Bay Area* by Chris C. Fisher and Joseph Morlan. The statistics about Domestic Violence are taken from an article in *The Huffington Post* 10/23/2014.

This book owes a debt of gratitude to the Canadian poets Roo Borson and Stephanie Bolster.

"Oriar" is the name of a song by the American psychedelic rock supergroup Heron Oblivion and "Old Snow, White Sun" is the name of a song by the Japanese acid rock group Kikagaku Moyo, from their album *House in the Tall Grass*.

Bio

Caroline Goodwin moved to California from Sitka, Alaska in 1999 to attend Stanford as a Wallace Stegner Fellow in poetry. Her recent collections are *Peregrine* (Finishing Line Press, 2015) *The Paper Tree* (Big Yes Press, 2017) and *Custody of the Eyes* (dancing girl press, 2019). Her sequence of five poems entitled *Text Me, Ishmael,* was published by the Literary Pocket Book Series in Wales, UK in fall 2012. From 2014-16 she served as the first Poet Laureate of San Mateo County, California, where she lives on the coast with her two daughters and Jimi Hendrix the Pug.